REGION OF UNLIKENESS

REGION OF
UNLIKENESS

JORIE
GRAHAM

The Ecco Press

New York

The Ecco Press
26 West 17th Street
New York, NY 10011
Published simultaneously in Canada by Penguin Books Canada Ltd., Ontario
Printed in the United States of America
Designed by Cynthia Krupat
FIRST EDITION

These poems first appeared in the following periodicals, to whose editors I am grateful: The Antioch
Review, The Black Warrior Review, Boulevard, Grand Street, Ironwood, The Michigan Quarterly
Review, New Letters, The New Yorker, The Paris Review, *and* The Threepenny Review.
*Grateful acknowledgment is due also to the Whiting Foundation for a grant which afforded me a
measure of freedom; and to the University of Iowa for all kinds of generosity—institutional and
personal—and particularly to Frank Conroy, Connie Brothers, and especially Deb West.*
To Anna Most, Brighde Mullins, Christopher Davis and Mark Levine, love and thanks.

Library of Congress Cataloging-in-Publication Data
Graham, Jorie, 1950–
Region of unlikeness / Jorie Graham.—1st ed.
p. cm.—(American poetry series)
I. Title. II. Series.
PS3557.R214R45   1991   90-13792   CIP
811'.54—dc20
ISBN 0-88001-271-4

The text of this book is set in Electra, with Fairfield display.

FOR JIM AND EM

CONTENTS

FOREWORD

1

And being thus admonished to return to myself, I entered into my inner-most being. I was able to do this because you were my helper. I entered into myself . . . and by my soul's eye, such as it was, I saw above the eye of my soul, above my mind, an unchangeable light. . . . I trembled with love and awe, and found myself to be far from you in a region of unlikeness.

(AUGUSTINE, *Confessions*)

2

But I was intent upon things that are contained in space, and in them I found no place to rest.

(AUGUSTINE, *Confessions*)

3

You hear what we speak by the fleshly sense, and you do not want the syllables to stand where they are; rather you want them to fly away so that others may come and you may hear a whole sentence. So it is with all things that make up a whole by the succession of parts; such a whole would please us much more if all the parts could be perceived at once rather than in succession.

(AUGUSTINE, *Confessions*)

4

Then the mind compared these words sounding in time with your eternal Word in its silence and said, "It is different, it is far different. These words are far behind me. They do not exist. . . ."

(AUGUSTINE, *Confessions*)

5

*That we have still not come face to face . . . that we are still not thinking,
is by no means only because man does not yet turn sufficiently toward that
which, by origin and innately, desires to be thought about. . . . Rather,
that we are still not thinking stems from the fact that the thing itself that
must be thought about turns away from man, has turned away long ago.*
(HEIDEGGER, *What Is Called Thinking*)

6

*What withdraws from us, draws us along by its very withdrawal, whether or
not we become aware of it. Once we are drawn into the withdrawal, we are
drawing toward what attracts us by its withdrawal. And once we, being so
attracted, are drawing toward what withdraws, our essential nature already
bears the stamp of "drawing toward" . . . We are who we are by pointing in
that direction.*
(HEIDEGGER, *What Is Called Thinking*)

7

*And what withdraws in such a manner keeps and develops its own, incom-
parable nearness—*
(HEIDEGGER, *What Is Called Thinking*)

8

To whom then will ye liken me, or shall I be equal? saith the Holy One.
(ISAIAH, 40, 25)

9

*And there appeared a great wonder in heaven; a woman clothed with the
sun, and the moon under her feet, and upon her head a crown of twelve
stars: / And she being with child cried, travailing in birth, and pained to be
delivered. / . . . And the dragon stood before the woman which was ready to
be delivered, for to devour her child as soon as it was born. / And she
brought forth a man child, who was to rule all nations with a rod of iron:
and her child was caught up into God, and to his throne. / And the woman
fled into the wilderness, where she hath a place prepared of God that they
should feed her there a thousand two hundred and three score days. / And
to the woman were given two wings of a great eagle, that she might fly into
the wilderness, into her place, where she is nourished for a time, and times,
a half a time.*

(REVELATIONS, 12, 1–4)

10

"Swim away from me, do ye?" murmured Ahab.

(MELVILLE, *Moby-Dick*)

I

FISSION

The real electric lights light upon the full-sized
screen
   on which the greater-than-life-size girl appears,
almost nude on the lawn—sprinklers on—
   voice-over her mother calling her name out—loud—
camera angle giving her lowered lids their full
   expanse—a desert—as they rise

out of the shabby annihilation,
   out of the possibility of never-having-been-seen,
and rise,
   till the glance is let loose into the auditorium,
and the man who has just stopped in his tracks
   looks down
for the first

   time. Tick tock. It's the birth of the mercantile
dream (he looks down). It's the birth of
   the dream called
new world (looks down). She lies there. A corridor of light
                            filled with dust
   flows down from the booth to the screen.
Everyone in here wants to be taken off

   somebody's list, wants to be placed on
somebody else's list.
   Tick. It is 1963. The idea of history is being
outmaneuvered.
   So that as the houselights come on—midscene—
not quite killing the picture which keeps flowing beneath,

3

a man comes running down the aisle
asking for our attention—
   Ladies and Gentlemen.
I watch the houselights lap against the other light—the tunnel
   of image-making dots licking the white sheet awake—
a man, a girl, her desperate mother—daisies growing in the
                                   corner—

I watch the light from our real place
suck the arm of screen-building light into itself
   until the gesture of the magic forearm frays,
and the story up there grays, pales—them almost lepers now,
                              saints, such
white on their flesh in
   patches—her thighs like receipts slapped down on a
                         slim silver tray,

her eyes as she lowers the heart-shaped shades,
   as the glance glides over what used to be the open,
the free,
   as the glance moves, pianissimo, over the glint of day,
over the sprinkler, the mother's voice shrieking like a grappling
   hook,
the grass blades aflame with being-seen, here on the out-

   skirts. . . . You can almost hear the click at the heart of
                        the silence
where the turnstile shuts and he's *in*—our hero—
   the moment spoked,
our gaze on her fifteen-foot eyes,

the man hoarse now as he waves his arms,
as he screams to the booth to cut it, cut the sound,
    and the sound is cut,
and her sun-barred shoulders are left to turn

soundless as they accompany
    her neck, her face, the
looking-up.
    Now the theater's skylight is opened and noon slides in.
I watch as it overpowers the electric lights,
    whiting the story out one layer further

till it's just a smoldering of whites
    where she sits up, and her stretch of flesh
is just a roiling up of graynesses,
    vague stutterings of
light with motion in them, bits of moving zeros

in the infinite virtuality of light,
    some *likeness* in it but not particulate,
a grave of possible shapes called *likeness*—see it?—something
    scrawling up there that could be skin or daylight or even

the expressway now that he's gotten her to leave with him—
    (it happened rather fast) (do you recall)—

the man up front screaming the President's been shot, waving
    his hat, slamming one hand flat
over the open
    to somehow get
our attention,

in Dallas, behind him the scorcher—whites, grays,
    laying themselves across his face—
him like a beggar in front of us, holding his hat—
    I don't recall what I did,
I don't recall what the right thing to do would be,
    I wanted someone to love. . . .

    There is a way she lay down on that lawn
to begin with,
    in the heart of the sprinklers,
before the mother's call,
    before the man's shadow laid itself down,

there is a way to not yet be wanted,

    there is a way to lie there at twenty-four frames
per second—no faster—
    not at the speed of plot,
not at the speed of desire—

    the road out—expressway—hotels—motels—
no telling what we'll have to see next,
    no telling what all we'll have to want next
(right past the stunned rows of houses),
    no telling what on earth we'll have to marry marry marry. . . .

Where the three lights merged:
    where the image licked my small body from the front, the story
                                        playing
all over my face my
    forwardness,

where the electric lights took up the back and sides,
    the unwavering houselights,
seasonless,

    where the long thin arm of day came in from the top
to touch my head,
    reaching down along my staring face—
where they flared up around my body unable to

merge into each other
    over my likeness,
slamming down one side of me, unquenchable—here static

    there flaming—
sifting grays into other grays—
    mixing the split second into the long haul—
flanking me—undressing something there where my
    body is
though not my body—
    where they play on the field of my willingness,

where they kiss and brood, filtering each other to no avail,
    all over my solo
appearance,
    bits smoldering under the shadows I make—
and aimlessly—what we call *free*—there

the immobilism sets in,
    the being-in-place more alive than the being,
my father sobbing beside me, the man on the stage
    screaming, the woman behind us starting to

pray,
    the immobilism, the being-in-place more alive than

the being,
    the squad car now faintly visible on the screen
starting the chase up,
    all over my countenance,
the velvet armrest at my fingers, the dollar bill

in my hand,
    choice the thing that wrecks the sensuous here the glorious
                                        here—
that wrecks the beauty,
    choice the move that rips the wrappings of light, the
                           ever-tighter wrappings

of the layers of the
    real: what is, what also is, what might be that is,
what could have been that is, what
    might have been that is, what I say that is,
what the words say that is,
    what you imagine the words say that is—Don't move, don't

wreck the shroud, don't move—

AT THE CABARET *NOW*

The Americans are lonely. They don't know what happened.
They're still up and there's all this time yet to kill.
The musicians are still being paid so they keep on.
The sax pants up the ladder, up.
They want to be happy. They want to just let the notes
come on, the mortal wounds, it's all been
paid for so what the hell, each breath going up, up,
them thinking of course Will he make it How far can he
go? Skill, the prince of the kingdom, there at *his* table
now.
Is there some other master, also there, at a
back table, a regular, one we can't make out
but whom the headwaiter knows, the one who never
applauds?
So that it's not about the ending, you see, or where to go
from here.
It's about the breath and how it reaches the trumpeter's hands,
how the hands come so close to touching the breath,
and how the gold thing, gleaming, is there in between,
the only avenue—the long way—captivity.
Like this thing now, slow, extending the metaphor to make a
place. Pledge allegiance. By which is meant
see, here, what a variety tonight, what a good crowd,
some of them saying yes, yes, some others no,
don't they sound good together?
And all around this, space, and seedspores,
and the green continuance.
And all along the musicians still getting paid so let them.
And all around that the motionlessness—

don't think about it though, because you can't.
And then the mother who stayed at home of course because her body . . .
Farewell.
Farewell.
This is the story of a small strict obedience.
Human blood.
And how it rivered into all its bloods.
Small stream, really, in the midst of the other ones.
In it children laughing and laughing which is the sound of
ripening.
Which the musicians can't play—but that is another
tale.
Someone invited them in, humanity, and they came in.
They said they knew and then they knew.
They made this bank called justice and then this other one
called not.
They swam in the river although sometimes it was notes.
And some notes are true, even now, yes.
They knew each other, then winter came
which was a curtain, and then spring which was when they realized
it was a curtain.
Which leads us to this, the showstopper: summer, the Americans.
I wish I could tell you the story—so and so holding his glass up,
the table around him jittery,
and how then *she* came along gliding between the tables
whispering *it exists*—enough to drive them all mad of course—
whispering *sharp as salt*, whispering *straw on fire looking at you*—
The Americans whispering it cannot be, stay where you are.
And the one in the back no one knows starting up the applause,
alone,

a flat sound like flesh beating flesh but only *like* it.
Tell me,
why did we live, lord?
Blood in a wind,
why were we meant to live?

FROM THE NEW WORLD

Has to do with the story about the girl who didn't die
   in the gas chamber, who came back out asking
for her mother. Then the moment—the next coil—where the guard,
   Ivan, since the 50's an autoworker in Cleveland,
orders a man on his way in to rape her.
   Then the narrowing, the tightening, but not in hunger, no,—the
                         witness

recollecting this on the stand somewhere in Israel in
   February 87 should You be keeping
track. Has to do with her coming back out? Asking for her mother?
   Can you help me in this?
Are you there in your stillness? Is it a real place?
   God knows I too want the poem to continue,

want the silky swerve into shapeliness
   and then the click shut
and then the issue of sincerity, the glossy diamond-backed
   skin—will you buy me, will you take me home. . . . About the one
who didn't die, her face still there on the new stalk of her body as the
   doors open,

the one who didn't like a relentless treble coming back out
   right here into the thing we call
daylight but which is what now, unmoored?
   The one time I knew something about us
though I couldn't say what

my grandmother then already ill

took me by the hand asking to be introduced.
And then *no, you are not Jorie—but thank you for
   saying you are. No. I'm sure. I know her you
see.* I went into the bathroom, locked the door.
   Stood in front of the mirrored wall—

not so much to see in, not looking up at all in fact,
   but to be held in it as by a gas,
the thing which was me there in its chamber. Reader.
   they were all in there, I didn't look up,
they were all in there, the coiling and uncoiling
   billions,

the about-to-be-seized,
   the about to be held down,

the about to be held down, bit clean, shaped,
   and the others, too, the ones gone back out, the ending
wrapped round them,
   hands up to their faces why I don't know,

and the about-to-be stepping in,
   one form at a time stepping in as if to stay clean,
stepping over something to get into here,
   something there on the floor now dissolving,
not looking down but stepping up to clear it,

and clearing it,
   stepping in.
Without existence and then with existence.
   Then into the clearing as it clamps down

all round.
    Then into the fable as it clamps down.

    We put her in a Home, mother paid.
We put him in a Home, mother paid.
    There wasn't one that would take both of them we
could afford.
    We were right we put him down the road it's all
there was,
    there was a marriage of fifty years, you know this

already don't you fill in the blanks,
    they never saw each other again,
paralyzed on his back the last few years
    he bribed himself a private line, he rigged the phone so he

could talk, etcetera, you know this,
    we put her in X, she'd fallen out we put her back in,
there in her diaper sitting with her purse in her hands all day every
    day, asking can I go now,
meaning him, meaning the
    apartment by then long since let go you know this

don't you, shifting wind sorting and re-sorting the stuff, flesh,
    now the sunstruck field beyond her window,
now her hands on the forties sunburst silver
    clasp, the white patent-leather pocketbook—
I stood there. Let the silver down all over my shoulders.

    The sink. The goldspeck formica. The water

uncoiling.
  Then the click like a lock being tried.
Then the hollow caressing the back of my neck.
  Then the whole thing like a benediction you can't
shake off,

and the eyes unfastening, nervous, as if they smelled something up there
  and had to go (don't wait for me), the
eyes lifting, up into the decoration, the eyes
  looking. Poor thing.
As if real. As if *in* the place.
  The twitch where the eyes meet the eyes.
A blush.
  You see it's not the matter of her coming back out

alive, is it?
  It's the asking-for. The please.
Isn't it?
  Then the man standing up, the witness, screaming it's him it's him
I'm sure your Honor I'm sure. Then Ivan coming up to him
  and Ivan (you saw this) offering his hand, click, whoever
he is, and the old man getting a dial-tone, friend,
  and old whoever clicking and unclicking the clasp the
silver knobs,
  shall we end on them? a tracking shot? a

close-up on the clasp a two-headed beast it turns out
  made of silvery
leaves? Where would you go now? *Where*
  screaming it's him it's

him? At the point where she comes back out something begins, yes,
    something new, something completely
new, but what—there underneath the screaming—what?

Like what, I wonder, to make the bodies come on, to make
    room,

like what, I whisper,

like which is the last new world, *like, like*, which is the thin

young body (before it's made to go back in) whispering *please*.

UNTITLED

In the city that apparently never was,
where the hero dies and dies to no avail,
where one is not oneself it suddenly appears
(and you, who are you and are you there?)
I found myself at the window at last,
the room inside dark, it being late,
the _____ outside dark, it being night.
Found myself leaning against the pane, the body beneath me
                                              naked,
and *lateness* not different from *shadow* around me,
and nothing true, nothing distracted into shape around me.

Outside, flashing lights, deep gloom.

A moonless enterprise consisting of towers not there to
    the naked eye.

Consisting of fountains, yes, but invisible, no?
And of what we spoke of in the dead of _____ once long ago.
And of long ago.
And of the fountains, too, no?, can't that be true?—
Does it seem to you, too, stranger, that something died?
Something we could call the great *thereness* of being,
the giant,
he who was a wrong idea but was,
the end the singleness like a gazelle could fly into?
See here now how he lies at ease,
the beginning of eternity he lies at ease he did not win
                                              the day,
his children the points-of-view are dead, they come and go,

have you forgotten?
And that the snow shall not come to unbloom him soon.
Can you feel them on your skin now too,
the layer of lateness and the layer of hurry,
and the coating of fear,
and the coating of the theater's empty now, dear, shouldn't we go,
(and then even the voices gone),
and *difference* holding the place in place.
Leaned against the window in the dark
closing my eyes to see that dark,
then opening again to see *that* dark,
opening and shutting to feel them rub against each other in here now
   (only in here),
the shut dark, the open dark—
and in between the _____ where the suspicion of meaning
begins, the suck of shapeliness,
as where this voice narrows now to indicate the nearing
of the end of
the sentence,
and the thin grief called sincerity is born,
and then the city that apparently never was,
the wanting-to-have-really-been, standing up,
standing right up,
and something else (the something else) starting to pool again (all
round) (below) hissing *bend down bend down O wretched wife,*
do you not recognize your love?

THE HIDING PLACE

The last time I saw it was 1968.
Paris France. The time of the *disturbances*.
  We had claims. Schools shut down.
A million *workers* and *students* on strike.

  Marches, sit-ins, helicopters, gas.
They stopped you at gunpoint asking for papers.

  I spent 11 nights sleeping in the halls. Arguments. *Negotiations*.
Hurrying in the dawn looking for a certain leader
  I found his face above an open streetfire.
No he said, tell them *no concessions*.
  His voice above the fire as if there were no fire—

language floating everywhere above the sleeping bodies;
  and crates of fruit donated in secret;
and torn sheets (for tear gas) tossed down from shuttered windows;
  and bread; and blankets; stolen from the firehouse.

The CRS (the government police) would swarm in around dawn
  in small blue vans and round us up.
Once I watched the searchbeams play on some flames.
  The flames push up into the corridor of light.

In the cell we were so crowded no one could sit or lean.
  People peed on each other. I felt a girl
vomiting gently onto my back.
  I found two Americans rounded up by chance,

19

their charter left that morning they screamed, what were they going to
                                                        do?

   Later a man in a uniform came in with a stick.
Started beating here and there, found the girl in her eighth month.
   He beat her frantically over and over.
He pummeled her belly. Screaming aren't you ashamed?

   I remember the cell vividly
but is it from a photograph? I think the shadows as I
   see them still—the slatted brilliant bits
against the wall—I think they're true—but are they from a photograph?
   Do I see it from inside now—his hands, her face—or

is it from the news account?
   The strangest part of getting out again was *streets*.
The light running down them.
   Everything spilling whenever the wall breaks.
And the air—thick with dwellings—the air filled—doubled—
   as if the open

had been made to render—
   The open squeezed for space until the hollows spill out,
story upon story of them
   starting to light up as I walked out.
How thick was the empty meant to be?
   What were we finding in the air?

What were we meant to find?
I went home slowly sat in my rented room.
   Sat for a long time the window open,

watched the white gauze curtain sluff this way then that
a bit—
   watched the air suck it out, push it back in. Lung
of the room with streetcries in it. Watched until the lights
   outside made it gold, pumping gently.
Was I meant to get up again? I was inside. The century clicked by.
   The woman below called down *not to forget the*

   loaf. Crackle of helicopters. Voice on a loudspeaker issuing
warnings.
   They made agreements we all returned to work.
The government fell but then it was all right again.
   The man above the fire, listening to my question,

the red wool shirt he wore: where is it? who has it?
   He looked straight back into the century: no concessions.
I took the message back.
   The look in his eyes—shoving out—into the open—
                                    expressionless with thought:
no—tell them *no*—

return to iambic s

MANIFEST DESTINY

(Note: *Rebibbia is the name of the women's jail in Rome.*)

(*Fabrice Hélion, 1947–1990*)

Northbound, on the way to the station, through the narrow
                          rutted
place in the patch of woods,
   the dust from the car ahead rose up
into the wide still shafts of morning-light the trees let
   through,
its revolutionary swirls uplifted in some kind of
   cosmic merriment, up

   all round the sleek whiskey-colored slice
of time
   passing—though perfectly still to our eyes, passengers—
a blade of stillness, the intravenous access
   of the unearthly
into this soil.
   The dust rose into it. No, the dust

   slapped round, falling, a thick curiosity, shabby but
extravagant, crazy pulverized soliloquy, furled up, feathery,
   around the
metronome, raking, as if to transfuse itself onto what won't be
   touched,
a thick precipitate, feudal, a glossary of possible entrances
                                     replete
   with every conceivable version of

change.
    Change! it seemed to almost screech as it rose again and
                                                              again
out of our drought into the stiff and
    prosperous stillness—*change, change*—into, onto
that shaft driven in firm,

    steely backbone of the imperial
invisible.
    I watched the stationary golden avenue. At every curve
watched the dust
    thrown up like some mad prophet taking on
all the shapes, all the contortions of the
    human form—bent over, flayed, curled back

onto itself.
    It was hard not to see the grief in it, the
cowardice—
    this carnage of fictive
possibilities, this prolonged
    carnage.
The gold bars gleam.
    The money is put down on the gleaming platter
like an eyelid forced back down,
    and another bill, and another bill, down,
onto the open hand, onto the open,

    —how long till the blazing gaze is dulled, the wide
need, bristling with light,
    unwavering, shimmering with rightfulness, god,

so still!—
 and the dusty money coming down onto it.

We rose from the table having paid our bill.

 Rome stepped back all round us as we rose up

—colonnades, promenades, porticoes,
 shadows of warriors, lovers and the various queens of
heaven—
 arms raised holding the stone fruit, lips parted uttering the
stone word—the stone child in the stone arms—the stone

 sword held up into the stone
cry—.
 I look into the air
for your face—
 a fold in the invisible out of which features
slip—
 until you put it on again, there, in the dusty air, the
expression you wore, click,
 among the shadows of the sculptures in the

Vatican arcade—3 miles of corridor we hurry through
 to reach the reliquary before it shuts,
to see the Veronica,
 your hands pressed to the glass till the guard
speaks—
 and the eyes in brine,
and the index finger of Aquinas,

and the burned head of Lawrence so black it seems
to face on all four

sides—then back out into the noon
    sun. *Rome*. And the word pulverizes. In the restaurant
you were gone so long I
    came to look for you.
Your face started up from the two arms below you—
    one holding the needle into the other—

white kiss on the brow of the forever waiting white maiden,
    forever and forever, forever and forever.
We paid up and left there too.
    The city even whiter now. White noise. White light.

    Walking the back way we passed the length of Rebibbia.
Cooler down there. Riverside traffic above to the left.
    We were used to them, the women's shrieks—hanging their arms,
hundreds of them, out through the bars into the steamy

heat—pointing, cursing, all the fingers in the dark noonlight
    screaming down the stories—who was killed, why, where
the children are, will you take a message, I'd do it again,
    I'd do it to you, come on, let me give it to you—thousands
of white fingers all over the dark façade, no faces
                                    visible—just

listen, listen and I'll make you
    come they'd shriek, trellis of iron and white fleshgrowth,
3 blocks long this queen of the skies—huntress—no face—

Regina Coeli

25

all stone and fingerclutch, white, raking the air.
You stood below looking up,
    the thing which is your laugh sucked up like a small down-
payment—so small—
    then taking my arm, hard, forced me to stand there
before them, below them—*here, do you want her, will she do* you
                                                    screamed—
    thousands of fingers moving—*tell me, will she do*—

screech of muscle,
    throbbing façade,
how should we make her you screamed
    do her time, drunk too I thought, the clamp of your hand
hard on my upper arm,
    the light down harder on my face, something rising in me
                                            as they
screamed down give her to us, let us have her,
    their one scream going in through
the hole where your hand gripped, the narrow opening
    through which I knew
that you would not believe in life,
    that you would hand the piece you were were holding back up,
the debt too heavy to carry,
    up to the balcony there, in full sun,

like a caress on the infinite
    this handing up of the full amount,
a handful of cloth, cash, skin—
    2:53 pm—Rome time—
in the marketplace now, in the arcade,

arms waving the flies off
over the cut meats, beside the statue of Caesar—
   two dancers with a hat out for change—
the swallower of flames, the fabric merchant

   holding the star-spangled yardage out on her arms,
and singing the price out—loud, clear,
   —what is love what is creation what is longing what
is a star—
   behold I show you the last man—
the price rising up on the gold track of its note,
   the cloth on her arms lifting,

catching the light, dustmotes in the light,
   and the voice thrusting round it,
and the unalterable amount—
   high, hard, doth she and did she and shall she ever more—
sleeps she a thousand years and then and then—
   a motorcycle through it now then a dog—
the last man grows, lives longest,
   is ineradicable—blink—
"we have invented happiness" he says—
   meats sizzling on the silver spit,
price aloft,

   perfect price in the dusty air,
us swirling round its upwardmoving note,
   milling, taking this shape then that, hot wind,

until I have to turn to let her voice in,

to feel the blue velveteen spangly brocade,
the invisible sum with its blazing zero ajar, there, midair—

and something so quick darting through it—
what will my coin repair? what does my meaning mend?

I pay her now. I pay her again. Again.
Gold open mouth hovering--no face.
Until you're pulling me away. Saying *love*.
As if to find me with that.
But I want to pay her again.
To keep the hole open.
The zero. The gold lidless pupil.
She will not look away.
Change change it shrieks   the last man blinks   we have invented,
                                               invented—

Oh why are you here on this earth, you—*you*—swarming, swirling,
   carrying valises, standing on line,
ready to change your name if need be—?

DETAIL FROM THE CREATION

I'm in the bathroom holding the baby down,
    washing it off.
I'm in the old world.
    He's still asleep—husband—it not being yet dawn—the baby
screaming, bad rash, the water running.
    There's the bell-pull in the shower in case of

an emergency, maybe you can't get back out, you know,
    there's drums in the background
or is it voices singing in unison then chattering—but that's
                           another track—there's
    mostly the baby, the cries in the small green
WC, the hotel before dawn, not a sound outside.
    Somewhere there's the voice of a man called John

Donne and words in an order we call
    westward expansion.
Things are like other things. Somewhere there's an extraterrestrial view,
    click: Can I from down there, please, from Later On,
have a shot of a) the mall, b) flying the kite late
    August choppy wind, c) the men

    haying fast to beat the rain?—Don't cry—I'm in the
hotel.
    I'm whispering to the baby over the water.
To make a sound that's better than water.
    The dream called storyline still sleeping in
the smallish bed out there.

Then there's this noise in the street, distant at first—

men's voices, chant starting up.
I look out and it's banners, flags. A face looks up.
   They're pouring in from sidestreets, thousands. They keep
trying to make the chant stick, they do it for a while now, it sticks.
   There's the sound of glass breaking.
There's the clotting where voices push up round a car,

   there's the fire starting up, there's
something they're wanting of course—it's in the chant I
   can't make out, baby crying, water

running—I'm looking down through the slatted
   blinds. I can see flames.
Words rising up. An arm that's
   pointing? waving?—it's
hard from up here—My husband is up now—The man on duty
   says better not go
out, you're Americans, better not,

so we go down a flight to the
   breakfast room,
three chairs at a small white table, moulding all round at ceiling height,
   Ionic fluting in the corners and a frieze where the tracklights
are tucked, white linens, the smell of how clean they are,
   the silverware pale with washing and soft
from the years—

croissants, coffee, the clink of our using
   things, the chant at the drawn

curtains,
    the girl, black dress white apron, more warm milk
for Emily.
    After a while there's no one but us in the small
hotel. We go back to our room. I pack the bags

neatly, the man at the desk has no information,
    whom should we call? We wait all day.
Evening, the noise is everywhere so maybe it's safe?
    Fires here and there being put out. There's a guy
willing to get us to the train, doesn't know about the bags.
    We're waiting for him to show. There's a moon. A siren back
that way. There's

    a length of moonlight on the woodfloor, a long narrow
piece of it.
    There's how it's not pointing, laying its thin lick
down.
    There's the shallow yellow
of it.
    There's the woodgrain in it.

There's the guy and when he shows up there's whether to trust him.
    And how we say we can tell. We're sure we can tell from his face.

II

The creator-king as asleep, as matter's resistance to spirit.

Spirit as perpetually undressing, leading to a present ("deep into the lateness") where nothing more can happen.

But in the myth, at the beginning of *our* world
matter (god x)
wants to remain asleep.
He (it is a *he*) resists arousal. A war ensues. A truce (us) (now)
and he must marry change (it is a *she*),
beginning the long unwinding every step of which is *now, just now,*
curious small house
out of which the great girl turns.

Turn, turn, this is the medicine, it will make you well. . . .

Where we are now she's done the bright swift part, the coil has long
since sprung.
She's deep into the lateness now,
undressing.
She's standing in the open ringed with photographs of what
took place.
She wants to *feel* what she *sees* now.
What she sees is him, the old King.
Her looking over at him words cast against a wall.
The thing we call *nothingness* the sleep that surrounds him.
The mystery of *interval*—her push, his refusal—what we call
love.
Here they are now: here is the voice trying to surround
the words.
And here: the words trying to awaken
what they would surround.
Will she ever tire of his refusal?
Will he ever wake again and, leaning out, give birth to her

again?
Oh ghost adieu—Thou canst not raise
thy head cool-bedded in the flowery grass—
only it's not grass anymore, is it, but sub-
atomic instances, etcetera—farewell!
Would we awaken him again?
Would we arouse him further from the drowse?
The tree is "green." (This is the medicine)
The dreamy outstretched arm is actually . . . (to make you well)
See how she lifts then drops each veil—
is this justice? is *this*?
A voice is heard behind a door.
Oh what will make him turn, what want can *place*
possess?
Out there: look up into the evening now surrounding
us,
what can you see, what does she have to show
for all the centuries of this undress? patience? desire? the thing called
form?
How long can it go on?
What is there underneath that could at last awaken him—the fear of God?
the explanation of the fear of God?
And after that?
And if she's naked now, then what is there to take off
next?
and then what will Love do?

Keats ?

THE REGION OF UNLIKENESS

You wake up and you don't know who it is there breathing
    beside you (the world is a different place from what it
seems)
    and then you do.
The window is open, it is raining, then it has just
    ceased. What is the purpose of poetry, friend?
And you, are you one of those girls?
    The floor which is cold touching your instep now,

is it more alive for those separate instances it crosses
    up through your whole stalk into your mind?
Five, six times it gets let in, step, step, across to the
    window.
Then the birdcall tossing quick cuts your way,

a string strung a thousand years ago still taut. . . .
    He turns in his sleep.
You want to get out of here.
    The stalls going up in the street below now for market.
Don't wake up. Keep this in black and white. It's

Rome. The man's name. . . ? The speaker
    thirteen. Walls bare. Light like a dirty towel.
It's *Claudio*. He will overdose before the age of
    thirty someone told me time
ago. In the bar below, the counterterrorist police

(three of them for this neighborhood) (the Old Ghetto)
    take coffee. You hear them laugh.
When you lean out you see the butts

of the machineguns shake
in the doorway.
    You wake up from what? Have you been there?
What of this loop called *being* beating against the ends   .

of things?
    The shutters, as you lean out to push them, creak.
Three boys seen from above run fast down the narrows,
    laughing.
A black dog barks. Was it more than

one night? Was it all right? Where are
    the parents? Dress and get to the door. (Repeat after me).
Now the cold edge of the door crosses her body
    into the field where it will grow. Now the
wrought-iron banister—three floors of it—now the *clack*

clack of her sandals on stone—
    each a new planting—different from all the others—
each planted fast, there, into that soil,
    and the thin strip of light from the heavy street-door,
and the other light after her self has slipped through.
    Later she will walk along and name them, one by

one—the back of the girl in the print dress carrying bread,
    the old woman seen by looking up suddenly.
Later she will walk along, a word in
    each moment, to slap them down onto the plantings,
to keep them still.
    But now it's the hissing of cars passing,

and Left into Campo dei Fiori—
    And though it should be through flames dear god,
it's through clarity,
    through the empty thing with minutes clicking in it,
right through it no resistance,
    running a bit now, the stalls filling all round,
cats in the doorways,
    the woman with artichokes starting it up

—this price then that price—
    right through it, it not burning, not falling, no
piercing sound—
    just the open, day pushing through it, any story pushing through.
Do you want her to go home now? do you want her late for school?
    Here is her empty room,

a trill of light on the white bedspread. This is
    exactly
how slow it moves.
    The women are all in the stalls now.
The one behind the rack of flowers is crying
    —put that in the field for later—into

captivity—   *change to 1ˢᵗ pers*
    If I am responsible, it is for what? the field at the
end? the woman weeping in the row of colors? the exact
    shades of color? the actions of the night before?
Is there a way to move through which makes it hard
    enough—thorny, re-

membered? Push. Push through with this girl
   recalled down to the last bit of cartilage, ash, running along the
river now, then down to the bridge, then quick,
   home. Twenty years later

   it's 9:15, I go for a walk, the butterflies are hatching,
(that minute has come),
   and she is still running down the Santo Spirito, and I push her
to go faster, faster, little one, fool, push her, but I'm
   in the field near Tie Siding, the new hatchlings

everywhere—they're drying in the grasses—they lift their wings up
                                             to the
   groundwind—so many—
I kick them gently to make them make room—
   clusters lift with each step—

   and below the women leaning, calling the price out, handling
each fruit, shaking the dirt off. Oh wake up, wake
   up, something moving through the air now, something in the ground
                                             that
waits.

PICNIC

The light shone down taking the shape of each lie,
   lifting each outline up, making it wear a name.
It was one day near the very end of childhood, Rome,
   out on a field late April, parents, friends,
after a morning's walk (nearing mid-century),
   some with baskets, some with hats,

(so does it matter that this be true?) some
   picking flowers, meaning by that a door that does not open—
And why should I tell this to you,
   and why should *telling* matter still, the bringing to life of
listening, the party going on down there, grasses,
   voices? Should I tell you who they are, there on the torn

page—should we count them (nine)—and then the girl who
                             was me
   at the edge of the blanket,
two walking off towards what sounds like a stream now?
   Pay attention. Years pass. They are still there.
And the sorrow kept under. And the quick jagged laughs.
   And all the while underneath something else is meant—

the *ladder with no rungs* perhaps, or *things*
   exist?
Meanwhile the wind bends the grasses flat then up again, like that,
   and at the picnic someone's laugh breaks off the mouth
and comes to this.
   Waiting is different from patience, friend. This

is the picnic.
   "Unminding mind, keep in the middle—until" says the silly
                                  book where
"Shiva Replies".
   In the field four bluebirds land. *Flish.*
Then no wind for a moment.
   Then someone's laugh, although they are lying,
and X who will sleep with father

later this afternoon.
   The mouths of the gods are stuck open really.
They are sated, exhausted, and still they must devour us.
   After lunch we take a walk.
We walk into their eyes, they cannot stop us,
   we slide on in, a half a dozen human beings
with the day

   off. Their faces are huge.
Back there someone laughs longer than before, too long.
   Click of prongs against a metal bowl.
And you, you have to take this as I
   give it, don't you, eyes, mouth?
Breathe, friend,
   the *sense* here between us must be gotten past, quick,

as any stalk must be gotten past, any body,
   that the hollowness it ferries up slip into here, quick,
using shape as its cover,
   one of me here and one of me there and in between
this thing, watery,
   like a neck rising and craning out

(wanting so to be seen) (as if there were some other place dear god)—.

   When I caught up with them they were down by the pond,
father with X.
   I looked into the water where it was stillest.
Saw how each side wants the other to rip it open.
   Later that day mother came up into the bathroom,
daylight toothy by then,
      color of gunsheen—dusk—

We sat there awhile, neither reached for the switch.
   It was not the thing we call time which was ticking
softly. *Come here* she said gripping my head hard in her hands,
   both of us facing into the mirror.
Then they struck out into the forest one here one there
      wherever they saw it thickest wherever path or track

was absent. As if there were some other place dear god.

   Have you ever looked into standing water and seen it going
very fast,
   seen the breaks in the image where the suction shows,
where the underneath is pointed and its tip shows through,
   maybe something broken, maybe something spoked in there,
your eyes weeds, mouth weeds,
   no bed showing through, no pressure from some shore, no

shore? I looked in there.
   I thought "I should go in". I thought "I want the fate
to come up now, make it come quick, this thing that is

the predicate"—"is is is is" I thought.
The face stayed there.

   She put her hand out to the glass.
We both stared in—me in the front of her.
   She pulled my hair back very tight.
Took black and started in on the right eye.
   Put it on swiftly. Her hands smelled like wine.
She shadowed the cheek, held the lips open, fixed the
   edge red. She powdered, streaked. I

   never moved. Both of our eyes on the face, on
the third
   party.
Reds, blacks.
   The light started to go we didn't move.
The silver was gone. The edges on things. The face still glowed—

bright in the wetness, there.
   Why should the shut thing not be true enough
anymore?
   (*Open up open open* the stillness shrieked.)
Why do we *think*? What is the thinking for?
   When Psyche met the god he came down to her

   through the opening which is *waiting*,
the *not living* you can keep alive in you,
   the god in the house. We painted that alive,
mother with her hands
   fixing the outline clear—eyeholes, mouthhole—

44

forcing the expression on.
  Until it was the only thing in the end of the day that seemed

believable,
  and the issue of candor coming awake, there,
one face behind the other peering in,
  and the issue of
freedom. . . .
  Outside it's almost spring in earnest. The Princess

known as *Luciana*
  back from the picnic
has spent one afternoon of light on the lawn tweezing hair
  from her legs. More drinks. The women talk.
Should she marry the arms merchant named Rudi?
  Is hisses the last light on the reddish berries, *is is* the much

blacker shadows of spring now that the leaves are
  opening, now that they're taking up

place.

CHAOS

(EVE)

1

What is it shall be torn off and held up, hanging—skin
    with a face in the folds of it—for
judgment?
    Here is the skin of days in the one hand of God,
drooping, the face running like ink in rain.
    Devils jump away frightened.
Nothing scarier.
    Animals flee. The skin of *days*.

    Here is the skin of *waiting*. The animals turn back,
they can smell it. It stinks with its silly smile. Hands still on
    the long strips of skin;
eyeholes.

    Here is the skin of having been touched.
Where the fingers of others ran—stitchmarks, bleeding.
    The soles of the feet red
where the earth leaned on them, where it forced them to
    still it.
Where the fingers of others have been: rips,
    blood even though it's empty, riffs.

The skin made of the looks of others held up at the end of a long fork.
    then cast into the pit, the open eye of
the one God (the Devils can watch now)
    (the animals can watch) . . . What will He piece them into,
hundreds lifted up at a glance, some
    with the feet still on,

46

the waters rising up for a look,

   the fires ripped up to see shape begin—
this foot then that fold—strips sewn back together—
   air bending down to see the sharp new line,
where the inside begins to be sealed off,
   where the stitchwork is tucked under,
soil swaying up in a wall to see choices

   begin—an elbow, one mouth—
the bat-winged angels hiding their faces but watching,
   the waters rising, the Finishing beginning now, the garment which
                                 is closed,
by which the open is enhanced, by which the open
   is freed—.
The air rises up.
   The fire burns further.
The open, the open.
   Then the knot is pulled in, the outline, the

judgment.
   Then he puts it down on the soil, the thing made of skins,
its hands resting one
   on the earth, one on the thigh. The head back. The hum,
can you hear it,
   beginning. And the thing still inside him, the girl,

still there inside him, awake,
   wearing him tight all round her like this,
him sealed, breathing,
   her inside his sleeping now, inside the minutes, inside them.

Then there's the time the elevator stopped for some
reason,
   her in there with me, old woman,
deep in the heart of the building,
   someplace daylight has never been.

We didn't speak.
   We stayed there a while like that.
I pushed down. Pushed *open*.
   She wandered all night by then. Hid certain things—whisk,
radio antenna.
   After a while I found the path she took
by the wear in the rug—

a figure eight—
   one wing more pronounced where it wrapped all night
round the recliner he'd
   fall asleep in.
The TV hummed.
   For a while after them there was wind through there.
I went by for some reason,

door not even locked,
   walls bare, floors bare—a window open.
It stood empty for a long time then someone else took it.
   The other wing
wove round the low table with all the wrapped candy—
   Here have some, have some, gesturing towards our bodies—

I tried all the buttons—two unmarked ones.
　　She started in on the names of
ours,
　　the dead ones, the other ones,

　　the whole chain down.
There seemed to be no one to call.
　　I thought of how much air we had.
The names came gently,
　　almost one with the breath,

　　though they stuck to the top of it, they took its way
out, fast to the heat of it, syllable, syllable. . . .
　　Then she pushed her hand down onto my arm.
Then she gripped down hard.
　　The list didn't slow, where was I, was she starting over

or did it just seem that way?
　　She'd sit in the office all day while he worked, very still,
　　　　　　　　　　　　　　　　　　　smoking,
for thirty-five years,
　　sometimes me in the corner,
the spike-headed minutes pushing up round her,
　　up under the thighs, there at the elbows, the hips,

　　sat in the day like the day,
only the wrist moving really,
　　cigarette, two barely split fingers, the bone in them—
Behind the wall the men at work—
　　saws, stitching machines, the dry sound of skins
being cut—

and the mink that are sliced into ¼-inch strips,
and the matcher with his monocle,
    and how you have to make the skins of hundreds seem it's all

one animal—Further back there's the icebox,
    there's beaver musk marten fisher,
ermine silverfox bluefox redfox,
    bear wolf weasel wildcat otter, sable and lynx,
wolverine, lamb—
    In the mirror-room,

    there's the spot where you're thousands going endlessly in,
there's the spot where you're one,
    there's the spot where you can't be found—
Why should it come alive, the thing inside, who said it had
    to come alive?
Click of the lighter.
    Traffic way down there. The six-a.m. train, the six-p.m. train.
Not even the foot on her crossed leg moved.
    Try not to make noise,

    try not to make noise that will call them all in,
her look going out from her into the office,
    her look pouring out from her, nothing going back in,
one way sweetheart, here have some, have some more,
    sometimes a hand into the bottom drawer for a new pack
darting.

3

Because the hole that opens in him is the edge of matter,
the very edge,
   the sensation of there not being enough
—that rip—and then the squinting to see
   —what is it out there?—
out of which the taut beast begins to grow,
   and rapidly, the sensation of lateness pulling up out of

   the sensation of there not being
enough
   (as you up out of this now pull)—
rising up out of the gloam
   like a name being called—
Who knew we needed anyone?
   Once I watched at the kitchen window a long time

as something rose out of the end of night,
   out of the roiling darks rising and wafting over the still darks,
until folds appeared,
   and folds in those folds,
and tucks where darkness stayed, held,
   and large loose cloths of it which the wind saw and dropped

down to—
   Until some shadows were hidden (and *underneaths* began),
until some cast up twisting (greens?),
   until some fell back after being used, thinner now—dusts,
silts—

and the blossoming white Hawthorne rose out of the very end of night.
The earth turned.
  The earth spit it forth.

There's the god that locked herself in the tower, there's the
  one cast out into the hissing open,
the white pushing out,
  the white flaring and pushing,
until the whole thing steps out, opening and shuddering, thousands

of wings,
  into the early morning, into the late twentieth century.
I stood there.
  There was a hole in my head where the thing stepped in.
The hole grew wider.
  Limbs on all sides pushed away from the center.
Depth started to throb.
  The hole in my head ripped a bit wider.
Now there were acrid smells. Greens. Degrees.
  Something all round stepping back, away.

  The tree rose into sight. Stayed.
The question of the place of origin is not true, too slow.
  Love pushed out into the watching brain.
Everything changed, stilled.
  I say *please* and then you are real.
The shape took hold.
  Stepped free.
And yes it was a poorer land then.
  Birds everywhere. Chatter in the upper branches.

Clink of milk bottles on the porch.
    The mind with the white hole in it.
Then the mind stitched up again, good as new again (the breath).
    Then the knot pulled in, the knot bit off.

THE MARRIAGE

1

I'm taking the ashes from the woodstove out.
Some for the flowerbed? Some for the garden?
They float off my hand, it's snowing on the mountain.
"Whose green mind bulges under the complicated hues?"
I hardly even need to toss them now.
As if there were another wind, there at the edge of matter,
they float, they lean on something I can't find, they follow it,
skipping over what's too slow, there now beneath them,
earth.
A moth is fascinated, come closer.
Come, come, the trouble will not stop, pay attention.
It's snowing on the mountain.
And what are these the ash *of,* please?
Of what was shouted out between axestrokes (the text)?
Of the scent where dogwood had begun to open here and there
between the pine?
(*Vladimir and Estragon begin to cry*)
Of the hand lifted to shade the eyes
raised now to gauge
the height (*They do not move*) and is it dead all the way
up? (*They do not move*).
You look at something and then you look and then the body perishes.
(*They do not move*).
In E's painting it's the end of the party, dusk, the bride
still in her white is sitting in the green lawnchair,
cigarette in one hand, drink in the other,
crossed leg still swinging now a

spangly shoe.
Off to the left a small dog sniffs.
I suppose she might as well get up, don't you?
She might as well, no one is looking really,
here in the vague sweet chanciness,
she might as well, it's dark enough, voices spread round
that will not, ever, be
returned to earth—
the leak's only one way—
as the smell of dogwood now just opening will not,
or the actual shades of green that hawk
around, penumbral, that spread a bit, that do not set sail—no, not
today—
or the twenty-four hours that will not be returned, ever—
And would she tell him, really, if she could—
could it be taken *in?*—pitterpatter now as Flesh goes by—

Later it will be the world as it has become.
Everyone will have waved adieu, there will be just the two of them.
The hum will be the car.
And the night all round them, bristling,
and the silver bits of them now floating through . . .
It will be the world as we know it—When she comes down
he will be asleep drunk in the TV
hum.
Were you expecting the queen to reappear?
It is *relaxed as dirt*
this barrenness become a place—
Her dress. What should she do with it? And she hears other
hums—freezer, two different clocks—words will come later on (it's
snowing on the mountain) something to live against will come.
For now it's a matter of whether to cover him or let him
grow cold there.
Whether to switch the channels off or let the hum stay with him
there.
Whether to wake him and say words and feel the year
clot.
What should the poem do?
What can still be
saved?
No hint had been given her, there halfway down the stairs,
having come look for him, hand groping the lightswitch,
seeing the world there in its blue light,
her still in her dress,
and off-shore, way offshore,

arm rising in surprise to the mouth now (or so it seems from here)—
                                                    no hint
whether to waken him whether to leave him there the icon the
chosen one the only reader in his shadowless
desire to be the end that will not end—
And so it was to be (I could tell her) night after night
(am I allowed to tell her?) asleep in his sleep in the hum.
Come closer. You look at something and then you
look. She floats off my hand.
Wind takes her for no reason for
a while.
Coo coo says the dove, gray-blue, floating up out of nowhere, pay
attention.
(*Well, shall we go?*)
(*Yes, yes let's go*)
(*They do not move*)
Softly she sang a bit then went upstairs.

THE TREE OF KNOWLEDGE

Then I came down and watched the fire awhile.
The marriage hymn, the star-spangled fire.
  There was a flame that seemed a bluegreen claw
at the end of a sawed-off length of limb,
  —a fingery, pointing, grabbing thing
pushing right up out of the body it charred,

  all the mad reds fetched-up with whites around it,
swarming, bubbling.
  No longer any of the inhale-exhale you get in a fire,
long past the flash and excitement, no
    desire,
just this insistent thing, much hotter, at its
    apogee—hollow—quick—

  just appearance turning into further appearance,
click.
  I watched the claw a long time.
Tried not to see it as reaching. Tried not to see it
  as pointing, as being
released.
  Have you ever wanted to put your hand right in,

  to open it up and push it deep in there,
to make the *other thing* begin?
  Meanwhile the marquee all studded up with fear, buzzing,
blazing,
  me waiting underneath in the parked car for the one hour
  you took karate class, the girls smeared
    into the one good piece of shade

58

at the frontier of pawnshop and incandescent ticket booth,
    the red and ice-white neon strobe blinking over the whole
truth
    making us come and go like
dice being tossed.
     Now it's up—how much are we worth?
What does He want, what does He need

    to win this one, old man poking the fire, making it
air-up right, making the coals flame up.
    He turns back to the game.
See Him?
    He's got some kind of diagram.
I'm parked at x. You're in the storefront at y.
    It's winter so it's dark early and from out here we can really
                                   see you

behind the glass all lit up now and flat flat,
    nine rows of boys all raising one arm up
and thrusting it forward
    hard with a jump,
the cry that's forced up out of your lungs
    lost to the glass

    so you look lacquered, gold, mouths open wide, kicking in rows—
Do you embarrass us?
    The girls are to the left of you—The classroom's light
making gold rows on the sidewalk they can be bought
    out of—Mixed with the strobe,
mixed with the short in the marquee,

it makes the clot of us
    bubble, glitter—icy—
with whatever it is that must be given up,
    exalted or spit up, frothing,
coming to boil—they turn, they turn back, one stops
    to shout, a cigarette, hope, armload of

spangles, charms,
    all the wattage of the marquee for a flash on the comb
in her hair, on the chain round
    her thigh. No sky.
I kept the car locked.
    Class took less than an hour.
Here you are now in your suit as before,

    the briefcase with clothes in it, the belt of some rank.
What can you kill?
    You told me once driving home—
how frail the bones are at the neck,
    how still you have to be to find them in the wreck of
intervening flesh,
    how rage must not come into

play,
    how cool the gesture keeps you when precise,
how then you can see behind
    yourself,
how then you can hear the other man's mind.
    The edge of your hand—you held it up at a traffic light—

was enough—
    People walked by in front of the car.
The cross-street hummed.
    Steak signs bristled on and off.
The map of the city shined and shined.

    Can you read it now, Transparency?
Is this Your round?
    Can You see them in there now, behind the marquee, the rows
                                                of heads
with hands attached, a sob here and there, some with
    their hats still on. A hiss. See us?
Hear the slapping sound of flesh on

flesh? The bits of face lit up—eye here, a socket, a
    lip? Onstage a girl
is alone on the bed,
    knees bulging up, elbows,
the head up now then down, the hand
    sometimes in view then gone, a pillow I
believe—a queen size bed—one light above—the red

get-up she's wearing stretched on tight,
    the rear-end up, shimmering, what light there is on it, red silk,
                                                a shout
from the dark, a soft dry shout.
    When I reached for your hand in there,
when I ran my hand onto your hand,
    it was to get that other sense of flesh,

where touch is the way to disappear,
   the old dream of an underneath,
is it still there?
   I feel the very top of your hand.
I feel the edge of you, the souvenir.
   Ruffle the skin—gently.
Look down at it. Then close my eyes. Then try again.
   What if there is no other side to this anymore—

just skin, skin,
   rippling, folding under, tucked tight, taking
shape—rounding the corners, lining the
   singleness, opening here and there to let the
eye through—
   the sound of a moan now but magnified,

the sound of a moan in the speakers—
   the red velvet corridors leafing back that way,
ticket booths, concession stands—brocade, embossed organza—
   gold trimming, recessed lighting, rooms, rest rooms,
back that way, branching back, all the red foliage,
   more in every direction,
starting from this plush armrest
   with the reddish hand splayed out on it I can
no longer feel

   out to the four edges of the only known world.

III

It is a sad, hard but determined gaze—an eye

that looks out. . .

(FRIEDRICH NIETZSCHE)

SHORT HISTORY OF THE WEST

Tap tap.
   A blue sky. A sun and moon in it.
Peel it back.
   The angels in ranks, the *about*.
Peel it back.
   Tap tap the underneath.
Blood where the sky has opened.
   And numbers in there—god how they sing—tap tap—

and the little hammer underneath
   and a hand holding the lid true.
What are you building little man?
   What's it like, what's it for?
We're going now, you stay in there.
   Deep in, nail at a time.
We're putting this back down, down over you, you stay in there,
   and then the storyline which starts where the gold doors

fold over the grassy curtain, click,
   and then the *and so*—hair falling
down all over—and the sky on now and the red sun on and the sunbeam,
   and the thing at the end of its reach—the girl
in the room down there, at her kitchen table,
   the last pool of light on her plate,

and how you must think of her now—tired, or free,
   or full of *feeling*—and the light she should rise
to switch on now,
   and how she will not rise.

ACT III, SC. 2

sonnet

Look she said this is not the distance
we wanted to stay at—We wanted to get
close, very close. But what
is the way in again? And is it

too late? She could hear the actions
rushing past—but they are on
another track. And in the silence,
or whatever it is that follows,

there was still the buzzing: motes, spores,
aftereffects and whatnot recalled the morning after.
Then the thickness you can't get past called *waiting*.

Then the you, whoever you are, peering down to see if it's
                                        done yet.
Then just the look on things of being looked-at.
Then just the look on things of being seen.

IMMOBILISM

The eye in its socket sweeps over the withered field.
  It slides over the still place.
Stays.
  A broken branch where there hadn't been one before.
Down from the very top of the tree.
  Busy, the eye that cannot be disappointed.
Still, the garden,

  the seven dried peony bushes we did not
cut back, rattling, black, even in no wind.
  Quick, the eye dips into the disappearances.
Goes right to the edge of them, hums there.
  Tap at the rusted wire retainers, their crisp grid
drawn hard onto the packed

snow,
  tap tap where the rust undresses into a
shadow grid—emptiness there—no peace, but emptiness—
  the shadow grid on the same soiled snow.
Murky places it is seeking.
  Then up and sweeps, fast, for a wide take.

Is it a translator? No.
  Is it an intruder? No, no.
It is hard labor, this need to work the whole ground
  and *leave it exhausted.*
The whole time in a hurry.
  The whole time looking for limitation, the place

without promise, where the adventure is finally over
   and *shape* grips down.
But it is hard to know.

   The day is still.
The light is still.
   If a leaf lifts because a tiny wind slips
along the frozen ground,
   the leaf will soon be still.
Where the burnished triangle of the garage-shadow
   licks the edge of the smallest drift,

   there is a hiss and a dream only the fast eye knows,
the prisoner.
   It can run along the branches without their knowing it.
It can leap without the branches' being forced.
   Such a young god, it can astound the whole

   crown with leaps so right they are what knowledge is
and yet nothing is touched
   in that other,
plodding way—history—where the crown must shake.
   It will count the berries at the tip—snap—
it will jump to the shadow-berries to finish

the count.
   It lays the number down on the face of the world, the right number,
                                      down
on what cannot look back,
   it slips into the green bowl left out last October,

it persists at the sleeping green insides—
    Click along the top of the frozen milk in it—

softly, softly.
    Because it owns it now, it can be famished.
The two white metal chairs look at each other.
    The eye slams their strong shoulders.
Again.
    The thing that cannot grieve.
Something sits on the table down there. What?
    The little warrior darts—electric—

    out to the very end of the line—snap—
casting forward for
    the annunciation—
for the swift change into *thought*—
    Out, across the yard, past the arbor,
down to the withered table, gray in the low spot near the appletree,
    down, to the manufacturing, *what*—

    darker grays perhaps separate from the lighter grays?—
shadow of the empty elm across it—*what*—
    that the eye of God still holds
unless I seize it, what,
    in its doom unless the quickness lights upon it—

a loaf? no, how can it be a loaf?
    entombed in being unless I can make it
out,
    trying to find the front now, the face—

Shall I take thee?
Shall I take thee to the word?

It darts, it stretches out along the dry hard ground,
it cannot find the end, it darts, it stretches out—

HOLY SHROUD

Deadwinter our thornberry
   drags in every last cardinal for miles,
its berries finally
   making it pay.
It's never not this way, the clear promise

drifting without perishing into the empty lots
   where they live,
the stubblefields beyond the mall,
   wafting and almost perishing
into the other stenches desolation and cold
   keep crisp,

garment of signals and truths
   winding itself among us—fronds, dread,
sex and fruit—sour milks and the acids
   of tin—drifting, a prayer that matter
is praying, not really ever
   perishing

unless it's bit by bit into such waiting
   as these birds inhabit,
their readiness where one strain of it
   is finally
heard. Now they're lifting as a large cloth would
   into a corridor of sun,

maybe three hundred sets of lungs
   drifting in unison, showering around this single blade
of sun like so many

minutes.
Sometimes I watch them
     in the back of

the mall, threading in and out of the discarded
     photobooth, necklacing it, trying
to nest in the plexi face-plate
     someone kicked in
after maybe three thousand faces had leaned
     their images upon it,

unblinking, pressing,
     the one bit of curtain left
flapping into anything's
     voice. But they fold down again now,
down over the whole
     barrenness, limb by bony

limb, seeking the almost invisible stickiness out,
     making it quiver all over unevenly
with their bodyweights and tiny
     leaps, slipping from still to blur between takes
to keep their wiry claws
     unstuck—oh storyline,

down over the whole barrenness—

as when the face which is His,
     which is not our looking,
emerged (the thing not made of human

glances) (the thing or moment)
during the night of May 23, 18-
    94 and Secondo Pia,

having immersed into the chemical bath
    his last attempt at a clear print
of the holy shroud,
    looked down.
The darkroom hummed.
    The negative image took form.
A face looked out at Pia from

the bottom of the tray,
    a face no one had ever seen before
on the shroud, a face
    that was, he said, unexpected. A face. A thing
whose stare overrides
    the looking. He fainted. The print floated

    to the surface of the surface
where it lives now.
    So that when they pulled the shroud out the front
of the basilica
    and held it up, the archbishop's gold robes
flaring the noonlight
    like an hysteria,

when they held it up laid out lengthwise
    on its frame, a large piece of serge linen
covered with stains and lined with

red silk,

and it took ten people to hold it,
    staring out into the crowd and squinting up,
the sun pressing against the façade like an interrogation light,
    and down into every beveled cornice,

and down onto the tiny heads and bodies of saints,
    and the tree of life,
and the stone arrows in the stone flesh,
    and Mary on her knees to balance
the composition—When they held it up to us
    we saw nothing, we saw the delay, we saw

the minutes on it, spots here and there,
    we tried to see something, little by little we could almost see,
almost nothing was visible,
    already something other than nothing
was visible in the *almost*.

SPRING

When I caught sight of them, the secret lovers,
I had been watching the pink-edged white blossoms
   in the garden below
fall, once in a great while, off the black-limbed cherry.
   Watching one petal start the slow drift over
then blow off sideways awhile then stutter
   down of a sudden to the wet black soil.

Poppies in a bathtub. Glistening lettuces.
   Seven white iris along the far wall.

They were heading along the steep chalky road
   that bothers this green hill all the way down
late-afternoon sun laying their shadows out, sharp, long,
   sometimes running a bit,
onto the white dirt.

Earlier rain. Then suddenly sun.
   Wings to every bud, every latched-on sucker.
Each thing swaying from its tight home.
   And turning, and opening, because so held.
Spring.
   The green stain spread.

I had been watching—between the lettuce and the small
   hydrangea—how the white cat sits
perfectly still
   tracking the shadows of the quick birds above her,
and once saw her spring as if from sleep and not miss—

flurry of white—
then the quick head shaking the neck of the thing.
   All afternoon me leaning and watching.
All afternoon her watching the shadows

   flitting crazy over the greens that break them.
She never looks up.
   Hunts wholly by shadow.
Time and the opening in it.
   As if I have no place really,

   as if there is nowhere to go.
Sounds rising up now and then from the valley—
   a hammering,
intermittently a dog.
   Shadows of other terraces. Birds diving to feed.

When I caught sight of them they were near me,
   a two-faced machine of gripping
arms,
   him tucking her hair round her ear as they talked.
There was orange blossom, honeysuckle, in what we all

breathed.
   And buzzing in the evening air of small bugs lingering.
And cries where children behind the wall were playing.
   On the steps across the street a teacup of flour.
Three mismatched linen napkins folded below it—

And sun on the steps.
And heat the steps can keep awhile.

    There's the cat which is still, which doesn't look at
anything.
    There's the ladder still up in the tree they've found—
though the pruning's long done—There are its prongs
    sprung out the topmost leaves—

two stiff antennae nothing can twitch—
    There's the feeding on up of the non-

existent rungs.
    Now they're at the foot of it in a shady patch.
I know it's not my place to watch.
    And what is poetry to do now?
What is it going to keep in life that life is ready
    to shake off, sleek now,
starved?
    It wants to stick to the skin of the beast
(there's singing to the radio out an empty window)

    it wants to stick to the skin of the beast as it shakes.
I can see them so I shouldn't look.
    They have laid her purple coat beneath them.
They have laid their red and blue umbrella down
    beside them.
He has lain himself down over her and in his wrists

holds her face still for a long time.
The shadows are longer, they are all pointing.
   My shadow is stretched across the parapet and down.
It reaches across the road below.
   If I stand here, right at the edge, my long pale shadow
reaches them,
   my shoulders move where their arms move—

I wait and they are all inside it.
   I wait. Wait. We are all waiting now.
The shadows of the birds play over us.
   Everything is choked with being to the quick beat called
stillness.
   I close my eyes to feel the strange

   slice over me,
feeding.
   The washing from the windowline above?
The back of the mind?
   The event crossing flapping its wings?
Something is creeping over them down there.
   Something gray and filled with minutes is laying itself
                              down over them.
Something without meaning all beginning is smudging the
   green where their limbs lie and taking the whole story up,

a wave, making the whole love fit into its body,
   until it is not a randomness anymore, the large darkness
with a head to it,
   until they're a white hole in it, opening and shutting in it,

until it is *the feel of the place as they know it* they think,
    it's what the air feels like now, what being is,
it's not a matter anymore of where it comes from, not any-
    more a question of
how long it will stay. It stays. It stays.

When I surprised the deer the wind was against me.
So I was given a length
  of naive time, green time, free,
to be the sole
  witness,
her blinking in and out of the one ray of light
  sorting tufts,
me in the Walkman where the self-reflexive strings of the
                                eighteenth century

do not die down.
  I stood there, fast.
Wanted the arabesques of strings, the nervousness, to brand
                            themselves hard,
  onto her intangible
pelt. Watched the skin ripple
  to rid itself of flies. And the ray lacerate
the broad soft back
  to its infinite pleasure,

and her take a short step through.
  Up in the air, in the transparent unmoving frenzy, the mind,
oars beat softly in time.
  A head sank into a gutter (blood starting out).
The strings interpreted (the wind stayed against me).
  Mother bent to light the candles.
Flight of a bluejay like a struck
  match.
Then twenty abreast (click) (click).
  Then twenty abreast marching through the city—

and all along the strings, the strings, bawdy, winged,
    (trying to make sure it's a *story* after
all) . . .
    Barehanded they grip the oars.
The lower limb of the aspen shakes.
    She looks up—it is a she?—
and there is the angel sitting on the limb now.
    There is the angel laughing, sharpening blades.
There is the angel—its robes the *mistakes*

    slapping the taller grasses; its sharpening (the *good
ideas*)—forwards, forwards, forwards, forwards.
    She goes back to feeding, the angel is on her.
He is grinning and slicing the air all round him.
    He is testing the blade (the air is blue).
When I look again it's an AK-47 then it's a saber.
    Look it's a spinning wheel, a printing press—no

it's a run of celluloid in his right hand—he's waving it—
    it's 78 frames of some story—then it's the simple
blade again.
    How can the deer let him ride her?
The *click* is my tape going into
    reverse play. The oboe. The *thinking it's for*

something—that sadness—
    sluffing over the god: tree deer blade:
is it going to braid them up right this time—the good
    elegy—the being
so sorry?
    If I could whip her with the strings,

if I could stab her with the rising sound of
violins—
    but the oars continue above us—we are so small—
and the angel is floating above,
    and the angel is knifing himself
to make the laughter flow
    (although it's breeze-rustle in the honeyed aspen),
over and over the long blade
    going into the windy robes,
sometimes crossing through sometimes staying inside awhile,

    sometimes straight through the throat, then up the nose,
his foliate windiness laughing,
    lacerating the stillness with the silent laughter
(as the breeze picks up down to the left)
    (and she looks up, peering out) and the wind

    begins to change her way,
the angel wild now on the grasses,
    the tree above her wholly hung with knives—hundreds—
                            clacking—

until I want them all to
    fall on her at once—dozens,
into the lowered neck, the saddle—
    the wind changing round altogether now—
until he gives it to me—the good angel—since I
    thought of it: and she turns to

me here now,
    and all the blades fall suddenly
into all parts of me giving me my
    human
shape.

History!
    A dress rustles on the spiral staircase.
I lay my forehead into the silver hands.

DETAIL FROM THE CREATION OF MAN

Even at the start, even before they hatched,
whatever there was to *know*
    was gone.
The mother was there, one yellow eye kicked up at me
    each time I lifted—barely—the hem of sage

    to see. Five eggs were there and then, one at a time,
a week apart, three birds.
    Two eggs stayed there till the end of this story,
speckled with blue like this our earth
    seen from afar—
the nest quick with twigs, grass,
    woven in to make a stream, flame,

flame with bits of dirt in it,
    each filament a reference to what follows to what came
before and disappearing now and feeding in.
    There was a fire I once saw
which was below all thought like that

and left nothing undone. It was
    of gold mosaic tile and made a nest, too, partway down
its life—
    beginning at God's feet as hair—gold hair—
and travelling down becoming rivers, wheat-fields, the hair
    of those that have to love, their love.
It flowed, burned, grew, until

darker of course, and near the end, it turned to
    blood and veins and promises, all systems

elaborate meditation on continuum, moments of beginning + moments of ending. (+ timelessness?) — mostly endings.
cp Adam hiding ←→ Adam before consciousness → (+, presumably Adam in final unconsciousness).

go.
    Then at the very end it was, I guess, the lake
of Hell.
    But up near the top, somewhere between God's

hair and the serpentine gesture of Eve as she holds out
    the thing in her hand which is an open mouth,
or a mouth *opening*—discovering it
    opens—somewhere between or just after Eve it is
a road, dusty like the one behind our house,
    and leads to the knot which is this nest.

It burned at every stage,
    all gold enameled tile and fire. Not the trace on it of an
idea, but gold, unreasoning, something like Time
    writ down in scrawl not meant to
clear,
    communicate.
Where Adam's being made his foot is fire

becoming mud, then, slowing further, flesh.
    The rivulets firm into toes, a heel, in-
step—
    then hair on him here and there
where the waters recede.
    For three weeks I go down there every day. Some days
                  before the news,
some not. In case you don't know this,
    they're torturing five-year-olds in the kingdom of South Africa,

they're using their sexual parts to make a point.
    A woman testifies. She raises her right hand.
Next in line is the guy about the ozone.
    The Butcher of Lyons. The Pope beatifies Anne Stein.
Let x equal perhaps. Let y be the

dizziness. There's this story
    where we continue, continue, fleshy and verbal over the globe,
talk talk, wondering what have we done—and this letter is to
    confirm—.
Once I lay down on the dirt and, holding up the fringe of sage,
    placed my face at the nest, breathing in,

twigs and straw bits at my mouth. I lay there
    a long time. A bird the size of a quarter, very pink,
eyelids not opaque yet, breathed quickly at the height of my eyes
    —a breath, a breath, blue veins all over him,
him sleeping on the other eggs, her gone and watching me.
    I knew I should leave. I knew there was a scent

I left, terrible, perhaps sufficient cause for her to let
    them die—like a word that cannot be taken back,
so the ending cannot be undone—*that* scent.
    I stayed. Where in the fire is this, I thought.
What for, this tooth-sized piece of life too added
    on,

what for, looking around at all those
    woods. More under every bush. Pushing on into here.
Where the theater is empty. Where the lights are down.
    As if there were nowhere else to go. Pushed in. Has

of Kaney's
drowned
kittens

nothing to do with love. Her sitting there some days like a

clock. *You must go in* the something says,
    pushing its thumbs in through,
making these protuberances extend—*out, out you go,*—right
    through the fabric, *in*—A madness from the other side—A

sweeping clean of some other terrain.
    In the picture I kept of Adam from the façade at Orvieto,
God has just called them and they are hiding.
    He sees them of course wherever they are, but that's not
important because now He's looking for them,

He's calling and looking. He's pointing.
    They're under three bushes that make a small shade.
They're folded up into their bodies, tight.
    As if they wanted no component parts.
As if they wanted to be themselves the nest, him with his hands
    over his eyes, her with her hands

over her ears. A knot of flesh, they want to be
    the nest again, but they can't, they're the thing
in the nest now, the growing pushing thing, the
    image, too late.
Their hair falls over them but it is nothing.
    Their arms fold down over their selves,

tight—
    They hide. They are what waiting is.
When I went back there today the nest was there

87

but torn and rained-on, frayed. No trace of them.
A bundle of dead grass and straw. I took it up.
   I turned it for a feather, scent. Nothing. It crumbled in my

hand.
   But in the other panel, where He has just
made Adam—the moment of his making—
   Adam has not yet wakened into his madeness. His hands rest
one on the earth one on his thigh. His head is back.
   The hole in the cliff

takes its shape from him but he has no idea.
   The cliffs and bluffs arc across from the standing God
to the sleeping man as if they are
   the gesture itself which they contain—a pointing hand—You, you,
be now. A tree grows up out of man's mind. An angel grows
   out of God's stillness—the heat He gives off as it

cools. *You*, he points,
   and the finger reaches through space, and the cliffs bend, curl,
and the tree grips in, and the angel shuts his eyes, and the waters
   ripple into pattern—*you, you there*—and the angel shuts his eyes
as far as is possible, further, and the man, the man . . .

HISTORY 2

So that I had to look up just now to see them
sinking—black storks—
    sky disappearing as they ease down,
each body like a prey the wings have seized . . .
    Something that was a *whole story* once,
unparaphrased by shadow,

    something that was the whole cloth floating in a wide
sky,
    rippling, studded with wingbeats,
something like light grazing on the back of light,

    now getting sucked back down
into the watching eye, flapping, black
    hysterical applause,
claws out now looking for foothold,
    high-pitched shrieks,

then many black lowerings—dozens—
    shadowing the empty limbs, the ground,
tripling the shadowload . . .
    Look up and something's unwrapping—
Look up and it's suitors, applause,
    it's fast-forward into the labyrinth,

    smell of ammonia,
lassitude,
    till finally they're settling, shadows of shadows, over
                            the crown, in every

                                \
                                ?

requisite spot.
    Knowledge.
They sit there. Ruffling. The tree is black.
    Should I move? Perhaps they have forgotten me.
Perhaps it is *absolutely true* this thing in the tree
                             above me?
    Perhaps as they hang on hang on it is *the afternoon*?
Voice of what. Seems to say what.
    This is newness? This is the messenger? Screeching.
Clucking.

    Under the frozen river the other river flows
on its side in the dark
    now that it cannot take into itself
the faces, the eyes—the gleam in them—the tossed-up hand
    pointing then casting the pebble

in.
    Forget what we used to be, doubled, in the dark
age where half of us is cast
    in and down, all the way,
into the silt,
    roiled under,

saved in there with all the other slaughtered bits,
    dark thick fabric of the underneath,
sinking, sifting.
    It is four o'clock. I have an appointment.
The tree above me. The river not flowing. Now:

feel the creature, the x:
    me notched into place here,
the grassy riverbank and every individual stem,
    the stalks and seedheads rattling at waterline,

the river made of the eyes of beavers, otters,
    of everything inside watching and listening,
the dredger parked in the river-house,
    the slap slap and click inside the water
the water swallows,

my looking-up, the spine of
    the x—the supple, beastly
spine.
    As long as I stand here, as long as I can stay still,
the x is alive.
    Being here and then the feeling of being. . . .

Everything has its moment.
    The x gnaws on its bone.
When it's time it will know.
    Some part of it bleats, some part of it is
the front, has a face,

when it's time it will be time.
    God it is in no hurry, there is no hurry.
It gnaws on the bone making minutes.
    Let's move
—but it does not move—
    When it's time it will be done,

but it is not time.
    I who used to be inconsolable (and the world

wild around me)
    can stand here now.
It's not that I am alone or that you are or why—
    It's not that we are watched-over or that the x's back
is turned.
    No.
It's that we've grown—
    it's that one must grow—consolable. Listen:
the x gnaws, making stories like small smacking

sounds,
    whole long stories which are its gentle gnawing.
Sometimes it turns onto its side.
    It takes its time.
Let it be so. Shame. Drops of light.
    If the x is on a chain, licking its bone,

making the sounds now of monks
    copying the texts out,
muttering to themselves,
    if it is on a chain
(the lights snapping on now all along the river)
    if it is on a chain

that hisses as it moves with the moving x,
    link by link with the turning x
(the gnawing now Europe burning)
    (the delicate chewing where the atom splits),

if it is on a chain—
   even this beast—even this the favorite beast—
then this is the chain, the gleaming

   chain: that what I wanted was to have looked up at the right
time,
   to see what I was meant to see,
to be pried up out of my immortal soul,
   up, into the sizzling quick—

That what I wanted was to have looked up at the only
   right time, the intended time,
punctual,
   the millisecond I was bred to look up into, click, no
half-tone, no orchard of
   possibilities,

up into the eyes of my own
   fate not the world's.
The bough still shakes.

IV

WHO WATCHES FROM THE DARK PORCH

With fire. Everything has fire. Fire is very marvelous.

Now we prefer light.

(OCTAVIO PAZ)

1

Is it because of history or is it because of matter,
mother Matter—the opposite of In-
    terpretation: his consort: (his purple body lies
shattered against terrible
    reefs)—matter, (in it
a shriek or is it
    laughter)
(a mist or is it an angel they strangle)—
    that we feel so sure we lied
or that this, here, this thing
    is a lie, a
sound, a
    vibration? Thing

so beautifully embalmed in its syllables,
    the orchard of them, sprouting up quick because of the sun-
shine.
    Don't blink and your looking will be the same as
their sprouting.
    Don't blink and your looking will go barehanded one on one
with the slippery, wrinkling, upslanting *it*, don't

blink ruddy impersonator in your gothic selfhood,
fringed with lashes,
    trying to match your stare to the orchard,
even as the possibilities (blink) begin to exfoliate,
    suitors surrounding her the one and only,
right version and more right versions,

    each one stripping the next layer off her,
her casting a look your way you catch and yet
    you too, because there is no choice,
starting in on the strip,
    her stillness suddenly not stillness anymore but the serpentine

flecked winking of the instant replay
    repeating endlessly the one idea,
which seems now lord like each time it's different,
    each blistering instance orphaned,
each impersonation, veil after veil, whirring
    —or is it *her* whirring?—
the brainfever like a shriek but inaudible, inaudible,

    and translating now into the mercury lights
through which the surgeons
    bend.

2

Blink. There. It's just the body. Put it on.
    Down on tight, yes, like that, it is somewhat elastic.

No hiss—no shame or crime. Monoxides, plasma.
   The carbon molecule like a great seaweed through it.

Hands, a lap.
   A sense of peril caked with a rubbery
forgetfulness.
   Waxy foliage all round for the glance to tap.
Inside, something angular, a memory of utmost
   rectitude—

   but far away, inside, like the reason that persuaded one,
                                        long ago,
drowned in the plump debut.
   So. Sit down, here is a chair.
Later there will be bureaucracy, heredity, doctrine,
   the "perfect" day,

but now, sit, here is a soft wood seat
   in the screened-in porch. Nighttime in summer. Hum.
Swarm of nocturnal intelligence.
   Cicadas unceasing in the confectionery air.
The leavening of milliseconds.
   Scurry of something in the leaves.
Laughter? TV through the neighbor's screen?

   Sit. The latticework and on it your gaze now.
Swank greens for your eyes to root in.
   Spores filtering in.
Green dust and the glance it's in, mixing,

green dust and the breath it's in, mixing.
Sit.
    There. It's just the inflammation—purr. Blink again.

3

Now I will make a sound for you to hear.
A sound without a mouth.
No face.
From across the fenceline, there in your neighbor's house.

A child's sound. Maybe laughter—no—maybe a scream.
The sound of a carnivore at the end of the millennium.
The listening also that of a beast, listening.
For all intents and purposes a shriek. The air sucks it up.

A riddle. The air is riddled.
It seeps through the green the cicadas derange.
The light from the neighbor's windows waxing the magnolia leaves.
Neighborlight glittering like gasoline over one side of
                         the big tree.

Now I will make it again, this sound,
from somewhere inside the small girl next door,
punctual, a scream, of monoxides and carbons,
a piston to what distended machine—a shriek? no? a laugh?—

lung-stuff, flinty, diamond-backed, floating out through
the layer of flesh, the layer of house, prickly light, pleated

greens, cicada scream, woolly creepers over the
veranda screen—a scream?

                              —isn't that laughter,
isn't that the cadence of crackling laughter? no—
isn't that too high-
pitched, guttural? what is he doing, our neighbor, in the cicadas, under
                                                              the

green, mossy, under the mercy, under the swank duplex?
Now I will make it spill again
under the milliseconds. Oh but she's giggling now?
She's playing with her father? It's hot. The end of the weekend.

Now I will make it impossible to tell the difference.
Now I will make it make no difference.
Now I will make there be no difference.
Now I will make it. Just make it. Make it.

How do you feel?

                              4

If I am responsible, it can't be for everything.
May I
Close my eyes for a minute?
It is so sleepy here and green, green,
                    the neighborlight golden-headed, slender,

stepping sidelong across the yard—
spice from his passage,

the lozenge of light over the treeflank and the greensward trembling,
where the flatfooted luminosity dawdles, substantial.
It is so sleepy here in the green.

Let the cry stay in the air like one more speckled creature,
interesting.
Let the pestilence add its color, no?, let the cry
float with its sharp metal wings
out into what it can't cut,

let it buzz out into the branches of the spangly
magnolia that will not refuse it,
let it be buoyed by the applelimbs, by the dayglo
apples, let it rub their skins, see how they

receive it, acid consonant
lofting in the spore-stunned air, magnified, slid under the wing
of the cicadas and helped to eternal life there,
pronged cry, wedged into the laminate grassy eternity,

locked in, the missing piece, the mistress of the scene,
let it coat me, let it be my iridescent sticky
stare—emptiness, green, and on it, instead of a face,
that cry
floating.

5

Maybe if I turn the TV on?
   Let's graze the channels? Let's find the

storyline composed wholly of changing
    tracks, click, shall I finish this man's phrase with this

man's face, click, is this the truest news—how true—what are

the figures
    and is this authorized—a spill? a leak?—whose
face is the anchor,
    who's that moving papers on the desk behind him

    there, below the clock, a woman? a map that
moves?, when the lights blink is it *now* there
    or are those troop movements? where day is
breaking? precincts reporting in?—
    whoosh—see how even you can't hear it

anymore, the little shriek, below
    this hum: hum of the set,
refrigerator in the summer heat,
    steel wings (the fan),
snarl of cicadas winding
    down,

whine of the bus,
    of the all-night safety light on the
garage (somewhere in here the

    problematic sound), hum of the anchor's voice
giving us figures now
    over the square where

chanting picks up, hum
    of the close-up where the infant's legs glow

gripping the father's neck—
    the lower mouth screaming,
the upper face squealing,
    a banner near them, and when the wind shifts,
a banner slapped over them,
    disappearing them,
beautiful!—
    cursive over their seeing—
black demands, serpentine—
    Then features pushing something facelike back through—
eyepits, jawbone—
    Where is this we've awakened,
the crowd is not satisfied, you feel the camera, the

pilgrim,
    slip as the reporter wonders
what to do, what's next?, the image suddenly elastic as he
    ducks—gunshot?—
horizon of stockinged legs, screams,
    close-up on a
sleeve,

then
    shape back in place, sky back in place,
point-of-view, having gorged itself, back,
    single point-of-view as if dumbstruck, back,
then the voice-over recovers, taut, its singleness

so thin,
green,
   like the bullet's path without the bullet,
a tendril, waving in the
   stunned air,
stringy, ar-
   ticulate, rising up, up, and looking back,
words its vertigo,

   all round it the hum of the crowd, windy, without

   consequence, a wheeze a snarl, dawdling, rapacious,

   the voice rising up, slender, no immunity,

   trellised on our looking, trying to root in our beastly listening,

then the image back, there, under the voice,
   moblike, throbbing,
trying to push up under the voice,
   trying to suck the voiceover down—
pictures, *the matter*,
   swelling under the quick
voice—

   the facts? spores?—flecks of
information,
   fabric through which no face will push,
proof,
   a storm of single instances,

confetti tossed at the
    marriage of

now to now: dots, dots
    roiling up under the golden voice—

    Now: connect the dots, connect the dots,
connect the dots, connect the dots,
    connect the dots, connect the dots,
connect the dots, connect the dots—

Feeling okay?

                            6

Said Moses show me Your face.
    Not the voice-over, not
the sound track (thou shalt not thou
    shalt not), not the interpretation—buzz—
the face.
    But what can we do?
Call the

                            7

                policeman, the surgeon?
    Who's the boss, what's the right number?
        I sit in the rocker, back and forth, back and forth.

Let's consider the dark, how green it is.
Let's consider the green, how dark, with the rocker at its
                                                    heart.
Forwards, forwards, the sirens shriek past.
Into this they go: thick sound of the rocker rocking: wood on wood:
so compact there underneath their going,
a footnote, no messy
                          going
anywhere,
            rocking,

erasing each forwards,

erasing—a sound like dice being incessantly retossed.
So it adds up in the end to stillness?
This the immaculate conception, the heart of the matter,

the great white heart,
pileup of erasures—play, reverse play—
the runners laying their equal sign down
onto the dry floorboards

till it's this clot, this white opening,
the scene of the accident,
part feather part scales—
                          thwack, thwack—the marriage

hymn,
what the god said to wait for He'd be back,
here in the place where it's all true so why move,

here in the nuclear-free zone, everyone in it for

capital gains, don't move, we can all fit, narrow place, He

said keep going I'll be back, you're on the
right track, keep rocking, forward, then the other forward,
the lovers in each other's forwardness,
facing each other,
both *forwards* absolutely

true—one of them death the other one
not but who can tell, they can't unwrap now, it seems like
it's love or at least a
private matter, they have the right

number, so sit still sit still the lively understandable
spirit said,
still, still,
so that it can be completely the

now, center stage, this your kind's
victory, the mind in
apogee—said *still*, said
don't wait, just sit, sit—Said

no later, no matter.
There, you got it now. You got it.

V

THE PHASE AFTER HISTORY

1

Then two juncos trapped in the house this morning.
   The house like a head with nothing inside.
The voice says: come in.
   The voice always whispering *come in, come.*
Stuck on its one track.
   As if there were only one track.

Only one way in.
   Only one *in.*
The house like a head with nothing inside.
   A table in the white room.
Scissors on the table.
   Two juncos flying desperately around the
room of the house like a head
   (with nothing inside)
the voice-over keeping on (come in, *in*),
   them fizzing around the diagram that makes no

   sense—garden of upstairs and downstairs—wilderness
of materialized
   meaning.
Home.
   Like this piece of paper—
yes take this piece of paper—
   the map of the house like a head with
whatever inside—two birds—

   and on it all my efforts to get the *house* out of their

111

way—
   to make detail withdraw its hot hand,
its competing naturalness—
   Then I open the two doors to make a draft
(here)—
   meaning by that an imbalance

   for them to find and ride—
The inaudible hiss—justice—washing through,
   the white sentence that comes alive to
rectify imbalance—
   —give me a minute.
In the meantime

   they fly into the panes of glass: bright light,
silently they throw themselves into its law: bright light,
   they float past dreamed-up on the screen
called 7 a.m., nesting season, black blurry terms,
   the thwacking of their
heads onto resistant
   surfaces.
Then one escapes,

sucked out by the doorful of sky,
   the insanity, *elsewhere*,
so that—give me a second—
   I no longer remember it,
and the other one vanishes though into here, upstairs,
   the voice still hissing under the track *in in*,

the voice still hissing over the track.
   What you do now is wait
for the sound of wings to be heard
   somewhere in the house
—the *peep* as of glass bottles clinking,
   the lisp of a left-open book read by breeze,
or a hand going into the pile of dead leaves—

(as where there is no *in*, therefore)
   (as where—give me a minute—someone laughs upstairs
but it's really wings
   rustling up there
on the cold current called history
   which means of course it's late and I've
got things

to do).
   How late is it: for instance, is this a sign?
Two birds then one: is it a meaning?
   I start with the attic, moving down.
Once I find it in the guest-
   bedroom but can't
catch it in time,
   talking to it all along, hissing: stay there, don't

move—absolutely no
   story—sure there is a sound I could make with my throat
and its cupful of wind that could transmit
   meaning. *Still* I say sharply as I move towards it hands out—

High-pitched the sound it makes with its throat,
   low and too tender the sound it makes with its

   body—against the walls now,
down.
   Which America is it in?
Which America are we in here?
   Is there an America comprised wholly
of its waiting and my waiting and all forms of the thing

even the green's—
   a large uncut fabric floating above the soil—
a place of *attention*?
   The voice says wait. Taking a lot of words.
The voice always says wait.
   The sentence like a tongue
in a higher mouth

   to make the other utterance, the inaudible one,
possible,
   the sentence in its hole, its cavity
of listening,
   flapping, half dead on the wing, through the
hollow indoors,
   the house like a head
with nothing inside
   except this breeze—
shall we keep going?
   Where is it, in the century clicking by?

Where, in the America that *exists*?
   This castle hath a pleasant seat,

the air nimbly recommends itself,
   the guest approves
by his beloved mansionry
   that heaven's breath smells wooingly here.

2

The police came and got Stuart, brought him to
Psych Hospital.
   The face on him the face he'd tried to cut off.
Starting at the edge where the hair is fastened.
   Down behind the ear.
As if to lift it off and give it back. Easy. Something
   gelatinous,
an exterior
   destroyed by mismanagement.

Nonetheless it stayed on.
   You suffer and find the outline, the right
seam (what the suffering is for)—
   you find *where it comes off*: why can't it come off?
The police brought him to Admitting and he can
   be found there.

Who would have imagined a face
   could be so full of blood.

Later he can be found in a room on 4.
   He looks up when you walk in but not at yours.
Hope is something which lies flat against the wall,
   a bad paint job, peeling in spots.
Some people move by in the hallway,

   some are referred elsewhere or they

wait.
    There is a transaction going on up ahead, a commotion.
Shelley is screaming about the Princess.
    There is a draft here but between two unseen
openings.
    And there is the Western God afraid His face would come off
into our eyes
    so that we have to wait in the cleft
rock—remember?—
    His hand still down on it, we're waiting for Him to
go by,

    the back of Him is hope, remember,
the off-white wall,
    the thing-in-us-which-is-a-kind-of-fire fluttering
as we wait in here
    for His hand to lift off,
the thing-in-us-which-is-a-kind-of-air
    getting coated with waiting, with the cold satinfinish,

the thing-which-trails-behind (I dare do all that may
    become a man,
who dares do more is none)
    getting coated, thickly. Oh screw thy story to the
sticking place—
    When he looks up

    because he has had the electric shock,
and maybe even the insulin shock we're not sure,

the face is gone.
It's hiding somewhere in here now.
   I look and there's no listening in it, foggy place.
We called him the little twinkler
   says his mother at the commitment hearing,

because he was the happiest.
   The blood in the upstairs of the duplex getting cold.
Then we have to get the car unimpounded.
   Send the keys to his parents.
Do they want the car?
   His wrists tied down to the sides of the bed.
And the face on that shouldn't come off.
   The face on that mustn't come off.
Scars all round it along the hairline under the
   chin.
Later he had to take the whole body off

to get the face.
   But me in there while he was still breathing,
both of us waiting to hear something rustle
   and get to it
before it rammed its lights out
   aiming for the brightest spot, the only clue.

Because it is the face
   which must be taken off—?
the forward-pointing of it, history?
   that we be returned to the faceless
attention,
   the waiting and waiting for the telling sound.
Am I alone here?
   Did it get out when the other one did
and I miss it?
   Tomorrow and tomorrow and tomorrow.
The head empty, yes,

   but on it the face, the idea of principal witness,
the long corridor behind it—
   a garden at one end and a garden at
the other—
   the spot of the face
on the expanse of the body,
   the spot on the emptiness (tomorrow and tomorrow),
the spot pointing
   into every direction, looking, trying to find
corners—

(and all along the cloth of Being fluttering)
   (and all along the cloth, the sleep—
before the beginning, before the itch—)
   How I would get it back
sitting here on the second-floor landing,

one flight above me one flight below,
listening for the one notch
    on the listening which isn't me

listening—
    Sleep, sleep, but on it the dream of reason, eyed,
pointing forward, tapering for entry,
    the *look* with its meeting place at
vanishing point, blade honed for
    quick entry,
etcetera, glance, glance again,
    (make my keen knife see not the
wound it makes)—
    So that you 1) must kill the King—yes—
2) must let her change, change—until you lose her,
    the creature made of nets,

    whose eyes are closed,
whose left hand is raised
    (now now now now hisses the voice)
(her hair made of sentences) and
    3) something new come in but
what? listening.
    Is the house empty?
Is the emptiness housed?
    Where is America here from the landing, my face on

my knees, eyes closed to hear

further?
Lady M. is the intermediary phase.
    God help us.
Unsexed unmanned.
    Her open hand like a verb slowly descending onto
                                    the free,
her open hand fluttering all round her face now,
    trying to still her gaze, to snag it on

those white hands waving and diving
    in the water that is not there.

VI

SOUL SAYS

(AFTERWORD)

To be so held by brittleness, shapeliness.
By meaning. As where I *have to go where you go,*
I *have to touch what you must touch,*
in hunger, in boredom, the spindrift, the ticket . . .
Distilled in you (can you hear me)
the idiom in you, the why—

The flash *of a voice.* The river *glints.*
The mother *opens the tablecloth up into the wind.*
There as the fabric descends—the alphabet of ripenesses,
what is, what could have been.
The bread on the tablecloth. Crickets shrill in the grass.

O pluck my magic garment from me. So.
                              [lays down his robe]
Lie there, my art—

(This is a form of matter of matter she sang)

(Where the hurry is stopped) (and held) (but not extinguished) (no)

(So listen, listen, this will soothe you) (if that is what you want)

Now then, I said, I go to meet that which I liken to
(even though the wave break and drown me in laughter)
the wave breaking, the wave drowning me in laughter—

NOTES

I

"FISSION": The movie referred to is Stanley Kubrick's *Lolita*. Some characters from it appear in the text. The poem also owes a debt of energy and texture to Tomas Transtromer's poems.

"MANIFEST DESTINY": The misquotations from Emily Brontë and Friedrich Nietzsche in this poem (and from others—Stevens, Keats, Beckett, Shakespeare, Donne—elsewhere in the book) are deliberate.

II

"PICNIC": This poem is spoken, in part, to Michael Palmer's sequence *Notes For Echo Lake* and so is dedicated to him.

"CHAOS": Eve is considered, in the three sections of this poem, at the moment where she is created and awake but not yet released from Adam's sleeping body. A number of paintings explore this moment. I was thinking in particular of Bartolo di Fredi's *Creation of Eve* in San Gimignano.

"THE TREE OF KNOWLEDGE": This poem is for Bill Graham.

III

"IMMOBILISM": Some phrasing is indebted to the prose (essays and letters) of Cesare Pavese.

129

"HOLY SHROUD": Some detail concerning Secondo Pia's photograph is from an essay by Georges Didi-Huberman, "The Index of the Absent Wound (Monograph on a Stain)," that appeared in *October Magazine*.

"WHAT IS CALLED THINKING": This was inspired by Daniel Simko's translation of Trakl and so is dedicated to him. The poem is, in a more general sense, a meditation on Trakl's landscape. The title is, of course, that of the book by Martin Heidegger.

IV

"WHO WATCHES FROM THE DARK PORCH": In section one, the image in parentheses (lines 3–5) is from Trakl. Section four begins with an echo from Czeslaw Milosz. The very end speaks to the ending of Theodore Roethke's *The Lost Son*.

V

"THE PHASE AFTER HISTORY": The name "Shelley" refers primarily to a patient by that name in the "Psych Hospital" of the poem.

VI

"SOUL SAYS": Prospero speaks throughout the poem.